REMEDIES
FOR
CHIRON

m. patchwork monoceros

radiant press

REMEDIES
FOR
CHIRON

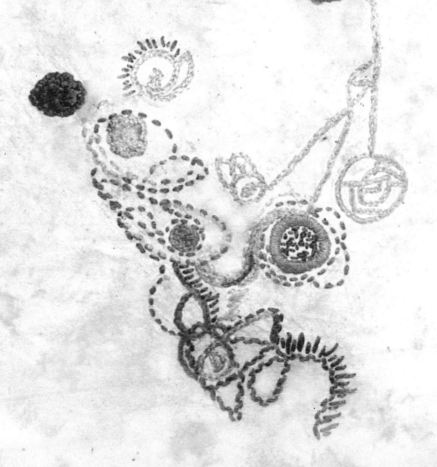

Editor: Suzette Mayr
Cover art: m. patchwork monoceros
Book and cover design: Tania Wolk, Third Wolf Studio
Printed and bound in Canada at Friesens, Altona, MB

The publisher gratefully acknowledges the support of Creative Saskatchewan,
the Canada Council for the Arts and SK Arts.

Library and Archives Canada Cataloguing in Publication

Title: Remedies for Chiron / M. Patchwork Monoceros.
Names: Monoceros, M. Patchwork, author.
Description: Poems.
Identifiers: Canadiana (print) 20230196020 |
Canadiana (ebook) 20230196063 |
ISBN 9781989274880 (softcover) | ISBN 9781989274903 (EPUB)
Classification: LCC PS8626.O5555 R46 2023 | DDC C811/.6—dc23

Box 33128 Cathedral PO
Regina, SK S4T 7X2
info@radiantpress.ca
www.radiantpress.ca

radiant press

Chiron,
an asteroid orbiting in between Saturn and Uranus
is classified in myth and astrology as The Wounded Healer.
Their astrological glyph is an inverted key;
suggesting that within our deepest wounds
lies the key to our deepest strength.
Chiron shows us that our individual wounds
can find refuge and rest
through the salves of collective healing.
– Charm Torres, astrologer

Content Note

*The following poems contain references to or descriptions of:
racism, ableism, self-harm, sex/sexual violence,
police violence, childhood and medical trauma,
death/dying, substance/alcohol use, and mental illness.*

Please read gently and take the care you need.

I

INJURY. ILLNESS. IMPACT.

3 • the m word
4 • Puzzle Pieces
7 • untitled fascia
8 • Twilight Tattoos
9 • Trauma
10 • Say Cheese
11 • An Education
12 • Seeking Afrotopia
16 • Smoke, no fire
17 • Looking Up With Feet on Ground

II

WOUND. WEAKNESS. WORRY.

21 • all mine

22 • C r o s s i n g L i b e r t y

24 • Routine

26 • Construction

27 • Holy Oak

28 • Variations on a Brother

30 • Refill

32 • dial tone

34 • Woman, Arrested.

35 • What Home Isn't

III

BLOODLETTING.

39 • pigeon
40 • Vacancies
41 • 570 Jameson
42 • "Baby Girl, Gayle. 1982"
45 • Portrait
47 • Lottery Numbers
49 • Mad Black
51 • Roaches in Daylight
53 • miscellaneous gadgetry
54 • Hives
55 • Bloodflame

IV

SCAB. PICK. SCAB.

59 • I Fell Asleep in My Party Dress

60 • Sad Clown Saxophone

61 • cheshire cat moon

62 • How to Fold a Fitted Sheet and Other
    Things I Never Learned From My Mother

63 • Down The House

64 • My Grandmother Keeps Losing Her Teeth

65 • mango threads in my teeth

66 • I Would Come Out Tonight...

V

SCAR. HEAL. GROW.

71 • Qrip Love

72 • nice to meet you

74 • Vinyl Spine

77 • Rise

78 • Deli Counter

79 • Sing Song

80 • with <3

83 • 2050

84 • ...at rest...

86 • To: mel   Fr: your indestructible self

91 • Acknowledgements

I

INJURY. ILLNESS. IMPACT.

3-5 drops of silence
broken into truth
take as needed.

the m word

Sometimes just writing or reading the word
"mother"
A throbbing between my ears
Sudden void
replaces the ground beneath
me.

Even with no further discussion of meaning or representation
the word just lay there on the page
6 anglo-assembled letters
swell my throat and sting my eyes.

Falls across the screen, the page,
the air just beyond my lips
mother, I utter
contribute to my own flagellation.

Puzzle Pieces

I want June Jordan to be here
I want Octavia Butler to be here
I want Audre Lorde to be here.
I want my Mothers
My mother to be here.
My mommy

Still in the closet to my father I
contemplate bypassing the
queer in me push through to
confessing

Yes Dad, I am poor, and I might always be.
I'm sorry your first-generation dreams for me won't come true.
Thank you for the money you say proves your love but
I thought love was unconditional you have a book of
rules.

I want to come to you crisp-clean
but you won't see the damage
don't believe this ache is for life.

I think of L who can't find a house to live in.
Rent-controlled doorways taunt from the tops of staircases
Beckoning bay windows, big bedrooms but no way to
enter.
These home-dreams are real, but
her wheels keep her locked out.
because this city wasn't built for her

Of A, who uses her finger to spell each letter.
She waits, with practiced patience for others
to use their voice
to ignite her words against the fuckery of poverty, her
daily battle for security.

Of R who limps and slurs
is Black and man
is profiled as a threat just walking down the street.

I think of how I can pass if I leave my
cane and the truth of my pain at home.

If I lie about why I don't work full time.
If I just stay alone when my brain crumbles
under the ache of worn wounds.
Each scar adds another era of weight to carry.

My friend the doctor tells me
she hates chronic pain patients
because they are all just
crazy
lazy
drug addicts
why don't they help
themselves? it's all in their
head anyway.

I think of her, wonder if she's right.
Try to count the times the men behind white coat clipboards told
me,
I made it all up.

When all of the neglect
inappropriate attention body
invasion mind evaporation
come calling all at once and I
c r a c k

Scar tissue seismic shifts beneath my
skin
I stitch these broken joints clogged with
memory I remember my mommas.

Fragmented shards of glass
eyed stares
I pinchslapkickscream
to bring myself together.

untitled fascia

thick paint layers of anguish accumulate
upon themselves in the fibres of my fascia

all of my parts attached to nerves have
bowed to their demise from distress

today encompassing sensation
sit or stand or lie down or lean or bend or breathe or reach or
stretch or turn or blink or move or not move or breathe or breathe

the joints and tendons in my hands and in
my feet feel both softly swollen and stiff
with crackling cartilage

I resent every mandatory moment of movement I cannot avoid
today

Twilight Tattoos

My hair was pink then.
You made me sweat.
I bled fuchsia onto your sheets.
Onto your skin.
Onto my own.
I branded you in blush for days we had stark
evidence of our secret nights.
Exhibit A smeared into the spot behind your ear where my tongue
made you sigh.

Cock-tip to cunt-lips.
Wrap your thighs around my hips.
Too shocked to scream.
Too stunned to cry.
The tears came later.
A hot, saltwater downpour floods my squeezed tight eyelids.
One more beat you slide inside. Fuck you.
Tried to break my body before you broke my heart.

Trusted you though. I loved you. I loved you.
loveyouloveouloveyouloveyou.

Trauma

Life with my nerves exposed like thrumming
electric thorns grown out of skin.
As I move through, nerves swing and sway
absorb each iota of atmosphere.
Sometimes, a handful of strands get caught
and tears revealing their sanguine histories.

Minuscule arteries drain
themselves of the blood that comes
from living every moment at once.

When wrong happens, splintering
my armor of ice,
crashes through neural scaffolding each
nerve tipping off the next.

With time they right themselves.
The wounds close, scab, grow over and
then, again, just like the first time,
the seams holding me together split.
Bursts through faded sutures
leaving me buckled, bleeding and
grasping for breath.

Say Cheese

Ivory tiles lining a smile that people keep telling you goes on for a mile. If I had a dime, gave a damn, every time I'm tellin' ya I'd be a Rockafella'. Shielding their eyes people try and disguise as they stare at the glare from my mouth. Keep it quiet, I tried it. No luck. I'm fucked at the first word I let trickle through. Not always so, oh no! Once, these Chiclet's were tricked out in diamonds. Stainless steel tracks closed the cracks, pulled the gaps; squeezed the skull to model perfection. Three phases of facial, realigning the spatial - first crooked, then cracking, now classic. A mix of some dough, doe eyes to my daddy and Cheese! Is what's left to say? Tight-lipped when I can but I slip, fall, and land on the privilege of flawless incisors. But when I see my pops, I'll drop open those chops to make sure he spies his investment. If I had a dime, gave a damn, every time I'm tellin' ya I'd be a Rockafella' And I'd gather that coin, take a breath, girder loins and pay back my tooth benefacta'.

An Education

Institutional ignorance releases slivers of my teeth as I grind my molars into dust Monday to Thursday. Week one. Establish yourself as an oddity, a lone black bean submerged in a dish of mashed potatoes. Weak one. Sadness, pure and irrefutable, at the life I have landed in, the life that is not what I had so carefully planned for. Louise Erdrich on the CBC. 1 in 3 Native women will experience some form of sexual violence. I don't know the statistics for Black women, but I bet it is not far behind. I hate living this way. Every occasion of me walking after dark stimulates my nighttime refrain "Don't get raped, don't get raped, don't get raped." Weak, too. Every school day my body engages, tenses at trying to defend myself against the subtle attacks of downpression that rain upon and around me in this institution based on ignorance, marauding as education.

Seeking Afrotopia

things that are hard:
- living with someone who hates you.
every day, often multiple times, you are assured that there is
something so abhorrent about your very existence that the
person you share space with is compelled to avoid you in any way.

every time your body nears theirs, your movement creates noise
or your presence is detected,
their scoff, grimace, recoil
heralds you as the villain

villains who don't deserve to have their side heard
villains' needs don't deserve to be cared for
villains are selfish and don't deserve anything they want

living with someone who hates you is hard because
the fragility of silence depends on soundproofing
made of ash and disturbed
by a breath or a foot step

living with someone who hates you is hard because
Their skillful front-facing masquerade assures an omission
of outside observation.

with every scowl on the staircase or reassertion of object
ownership you're reminded that you are not trustworthy
every time a mug, a sweater, a snack of theirs appears to be
missing
every time a cupboard, shelf, appliance
that was once shared, becomes separate
you're told you make them feel unsafe.

because no matter your efforts to ghostly float around
the periphery of their perception;
even when you stop making tea and toast, smoothies,
any meals needing more than one pot
because you're afraid of forgetting a cup or a fork or a crumpled
wrapper behind, of being too ill or worn out to tidy right away
even when you start bringing the takeout directly to your
basement room, always asking for extra cutlery
despite the roach odour still offgassing from your recent
infestation and the anxiety that ignites

even when you push through to do chores that have
never fit your capacity;
when you carry hefts up and down stairs,
vacuum multiple rooms and levels,
use products that invite migraines and cognitive breakdowns

even when you start losing weight because you spend more
time retracted into yourself, listening for what mood the tone
of their footsteps implies, than you do thinking about eating
making any sound including chewing begins to feel dangerous
and antagonistic

even when you start pulling out your hair
plucking each one out at the root
running your fingers over the smoothness left behind
leaving piles of perfectly kinked curls on your pillow

even when there is so little of you to notice

one glint of eye contact
either wayward or intentional
one meekly raised concern or boundary
dissolves the masterfully renegotiated terms of your
will to live

You are horrific.

You're so horrific, I don't want your fork on my plate, much less your almond milk and my half and half touching on the same shelf of the fridge.

You're so horrific, I am repulsed by even the echo of your corporeal proximity.

When you're so small, the indent on your pillow becomes the only proof of your personhood.

That I get to move out
in a month
in a year
when I'm grown

That I am loved
may be missed
by my cats
by my friends
by my other relatives

That we're both Black
That it's my house too
That they asked me to live here
That they told me to grow up here

None of this matters,
because when you live with someone who hates you

Every minute is a performance to placate their hatred.

Every hour is a mirror showing the reflection of the parts of you they'll never want.

Every day you wonder what happens if your tolerance peaks, but you still can't leave.

Every night you go to bed uncertain if the person in the next room would carry you to safety in case of a fire.

Every morning you utter under your breath thanks to the universe that you made it through another sleep, without your body being left to burn.

Smoke, no fire

Great grey billows swirl in the
caverns behind their eyes
Soot stains the skull of a girl
who has fallen,
and cannot rise.

A serpentine tendril, reaching, wisping and whirling by altitude
and air currents.

Looking Up With Feet on Ground

(1)
Perpetually preparing for take-off,
Our authentic agricultural architecture
Slides up the cityscape,
Drops into an Emerald jigsaw.
Pushing ether between cumulus bunnies,
Those possible veracities dissolve.
If I pack all my luggage
Leave behind all the baggage
Will I land as a different me?

(2)
Our authentic agricultural architecture
Slides up the cityscape,
Drops into an Emerald jigsaw.
Floating with grounded feet
Her earthen awareness dissolves.
Pushing the ether between cumulus bunnies,
Those possible veracities
Exchange their known ethnicities
For a seat number.
If I pack all my luggage
Leave behind all the baggage
Will I land as a different me?

(3)
Slide up the cityscape,
Reach a soaring altitude and
Drop into an Emerald jigsaw.
Floating with grounded feet
Her earthen awareness dissolves.
His neighbour, a stranger
Fell through an air pocket

Into a landscape anew.
Pushing the ether between cumulus bunnies,
Those possible veracities
Exchange their owned ethnicities
For a number. Next please.
Forgot to pack my luggage
Left behind all the baggage
I land as a different me.

II

WOUND. WEAKNESS. WORRY.

boil one cup of fresh tears
add dried leaves of family tree
steep for one lifetime, drink.

all mine

rode past ~~our~~
my
old apartment tonight

not ours

my upmarket basement apartment
filled with the mail-ordered artefacts I
bought while I waited for you
to want to move in with me
you never did

now all I have are things

4 board games I never play
3 multi-vinyl discography of The Beatles
2 Autoharps I didn't really learn to play to accompany you on cello
in the band we never formed
1 pair of tower speakers I lost the adapter for
1 H&M zip-up hoodie laundered clean of your aroma
1 copy of Simone de Beauvoir's Letters to Jean Paul Sartre to sit
alongside your copy of
Sartre's Being and Nothingness
1 yellow-handled Hello Kitty spoon
1 pair of leather handcuffs we used once
1 gifted copy of bell hooks' All About Love you never read
because you didn't think it mattered that you were white
and I was not.

CrossingLiberty

Barrelling through traffic towards the gates at the
lake,
a tease of freedom, ironic in their ornate architecture.

Ivory arches climb to crown the horizon,
an industrial sunset of steel and concrete.
Held in place by brick, and the bones of
dark-skinned workers whose names have
been lost to tongues no longer fluent in
ancestry.

The gates sparkle beneath a constellation of synthetically
charged fireflies.
Trained to spell out the colossal, conspicuous banner.
The search beams intermittently interrupt them raking the sky,
reminding fugitives of the law of the land of their minds:
The City is Always Watching.

"Welcome to the 2180 Canadian National Exhibition!
Celebrating 300 Years"

She squints her black lashes shut,
trying to dismantle the dazzle.
Even through the grey grime slicked
across each bus window, the city
pierces into her personhood.

Chestnut hands pull along their clutches of children, indentured
eyes lock lashes over leather muzzles and opaque ocular
guards.

An unspoken, "I see you too" ripples
between the gazes
of these golden hour
workhorses. The one in the
saddle and the one in the
uniform.

At the end of the day,
She will hand back her fair-haired charges.
Careful not to cross the barrier that separates her side of
the road from the side reserved for her languid
Liberty Village employers.

The bus pulls away
and the clear waters that lap against the ankles of the city
send off chilly mists.

She watches the gates shrink from view,
gradually swallowed by the thick green fog
mushrooming into the air.
Hazard-haze belches from derelict, uncovered
manholes littering the road back to her part of
town.

Routine

WAKE UP!
sore, groggy,
headache. play
bedspread hide and seek
with the cats
open the door
for the dog
but keep the cats inside
let the dog out.
distract the cats
open cans and shake the kibble
sneak away
let the dog back in

Water
for everyone.

Cipralex & Wellbutrin & Zyprexa & Paxil
Abilify to relieve the drowsiness (from the night drugs)
Adderall – to counteract the sedatives (for the painsomnia)

Streetcar
steps
no seats
"can I please sit down?"
stank eye and
"sit where?"
squeezing back tears
cramp spasm stab pinch
wince

open front door.

sore, groggy,
headache, hungry.
backache, foot
pain, joint swelling, walk
the dog
don't let the cats out
front door
distract the cats
shake the treats
chicken liver pate
let the dog out
homework
call the dog back in
wave the feather dangler
hairball
call the dog back in
again.

Trazodone & Seroquel & Gabapentin & Cessamet & Ibuprofen &
weed & Percocet & T3s & Naproxen & heating pad & foam roller
& acuball & orthotic insoles & wrist brace & ice pack & muscle
rub & hot water & child's pose
for sleep
for anxiety
for depression
for pain

let the dog back in

Construction

I've pressed my forehead against this glass for hours,
Hands raised; my fingernails reflexively scrape the cold surface.
A cool puddle forms around my feet.
Blends with concrete dust to form a sticky paste.
My brain is slowly trickling out of my ears.
Involuntary response to your incessant digging.

Holy Oak
(now closed café-bar in Toronto, ON)

The leg of this chair is loose, the chipped shabby-chic white paint
flaking off with every bounce of my restless legs.
I can see the sky above my house through the storefront
window and wonder what my cats are doing.
I sit parked in the corner of this show because I care for my friend,
but they've already gone on and I'd rather skip to the catching up
part of the night; or just go home.
I am the only Black or person of colour I can see in this crowd of
side shaves and button-up shirts.
I think this is my community according to the most recently
updated acronym but
Where am I?
Not a week ago I was deep into my gradually re-emerging
Blackness.
Settling into nests of my unfurling roots in Jamaica.
I was surrounded by a multitude of modes of being Black,
Jamaican, queer, poet...
Here I am entrenched in white/queer/transmasculinity.
Elitism chokes the air.

Variations on a Brother

Harold
The value of my achievements is disintegrating.
Heading homeward downward chin.
My daylight hours are usurped now by Lasers and pixels.
Returning home, drained of drive,
I am met with the perfunctory embraces and shoulder pats
of those I have pushed away.
Another deep breath.
Inhaling essence of damp carpets and warping wall panels,
The responsibility of my tandem position
Slouches like wet clay between my shoulder blades.
Sigh and exhale, a head held high.
A life, now a lie.
Threads bound together by force of will.

Jeffery
Today like every other I will wake and decide to start.
Lying in bed
Perpetually determined to showcase my genius.
Daylight whittles the time further from my purpose.
Uneasy with the peripheral intrusion of possible failure
Devilish doubts erode their way into my cranium.
Fingerprints rubbed smooth
Already coarse pads peel, chafing from
Constant corduroy friction.
I am the fulcrum.
Joining us all together but I
Have to hold the weight.
Recalling a flounce of blonde
corkscrew curls
Bleached white in summertime.
But no, today I will succeed.
Triumphant over my inertia,
Poised between moistening knuckles
This pen, instrument of my defeat.

Douglas

I am the last in line.
The dregs of my genes hang,
Proteinlace clinging to my bones.
Relations refusing to recognize
My indifference to our supposedly
shared affections.
Attentions and flourishes lathered thick on one and two.
What's left is myself
A teabag twice steeped.
When tasted first, strong and memorable.
Once more, faded but bitter enough to rest
Thick on your tongue.
Pour hot water thrice upon me
My emissions weak.
Compress tight as I might, my blood will run clear.

KIN.

Everything I have ever held valuable will start. Again.
Lying in the dregs of my daylight hours,
The Sun, perpetually gazing downward
Ridicules my genius genes.
Anxious with social barrier construction, my
Relations beside me whittle away my disinterest.
Lathering what's left of myself
Thick upon the broken man returned home
To damp carpets, warping walls and corduroy.
The weight of our bouncing corkscrews hangs listlessly
Between my shoulder blades.
Our protein laced bones bleached white in summertime and,
Head held high I sigh, triumphant;
Bind threads of defeat tight between my palms.

Refill

(1)
dimpled talcum powder
palms
reach clumsily
disembodied objects floating
in the front
of her infant periphery
newblue irises lock
onto the eyes caged in crow's feet
cooing to the voice
echoed within the walls
knuckles soft as sponges
grip tight
light blue plastic
rattles with chalky milkteeth
music
not made
for babies

(2)
gnawing through knots in
my shoulder blades strain
you left fingerprints.
cellular coils pressed to
dust
powdered relief in
the bottom of
the bottle   –

(3)
you hold your love
locked tight
electric blue plastic
under child-proof lid
partially obscured by
a weather-worn label
you take it out
only when you need a fix

dial tone

1.
sweat-screaming agony
she heaves.
filling the air with noise to quell the urge to
call
she clenches a fist to quench the craving
her fingertips repeat the rhythm of his number

she moves the phone further over there
not giving her eyes the vista to scan
that might derail her determination.

chill-shivering clarity she
breathes.

intergenerational stalemate
willfully sustained
she won't surrender
the image

brown knuckles stretched white
receiver warms evenly under
this nepotistic obligation

blood-thinning resilience
she hangs

up.

2.
sweat-screaming agony you
leave.

wilfully ignoring the urge to
call
you clench your fist to quench the craving
your fingertips repeat the rhythm of her number

you move the phone closer
over here

not giving your ears the chance
to run or to
betray your
imagination.

chill-shivering clarity you
seethe.

intergenerational stalemate
willfully sustained you won't surrender the image
will you?

brown knuckles stretched white
receiver cools, awaiting the unescapable redial
drawing this nepotistic compulsion to an
end
blood-thinning resilience
you pick

up.

Woman, Arrested.

Sun streaming through parted curtains
the brightness forcing facial contractions
that distort my vision, I blink.
Shift my gaze, focus on shadows
push my eyes past the orange, past the pink.

She was easily outnumbered, two to one.
Cornered, caged-in, pressed into the car I
look for her friends, there were none.

What Home Isn't

what home isn't a cage? wing-crushing
walls of barbed filigree; safe from the
hazards beyond trapped with the peril
within.

what home isn't a petri dish?
oppositional mycelia tightly compressed
an experiment of will:
observe which cell flexes osmosis first, absorbing their neighbour.

what home isn't a fairy tale?
spectral shadows wafting through locked doors
a lost and crying princess wishing to be saved
by the mother she never knew.

III

BLOODLETTING.

sprinkle three handfuls
brick-red sand from the homeland on
sheets at night, sleep.

pigeon

day three of the dead pigeon
in my alleyway the alleyway
to my apartment the
apartment where i live

rare breed of bird
buttercream, blush pink and sandy brown
spotted with feather freckles
lies tranquil on day one.

petrifying plumes
graze a concrete curb
yet untouched by passing
rodent teeth on day two

stride interrupted mid-step
a local call from this graveside in sight of my doorstep
quiets the ambient
city static of racing mouths and motors

more accustomed to long distance correspondence I
am stunned at the surprise ringing in my ears

Vacancies

First the crash.
Century-old plaster, rot, debris crumbling
upon my surprised self.
Me an unsuspecting Mx. Muffet
usurped again whilst in the low-rent throes
of urban-centre adulting.

Then, the bone.
Decayed remnants of an upstairs
guest?
or
hidden fortune of a ferreting visitor
squirreled away for later ingestion
only to be lost, deserted
ignored by beady eyes enraptured
instead by glimmering refuse.

570 Jameson

My great granny was a respectable farmer and entrepreneur.
My great grandaddy died early, left the business and the babies
solely in her care.
Alone with 8 children, the 9th already in the ground.
Poor Granny only had the crop to depend on.
Pimento and coffee.
Nobody no call no body their right name.
Died two weeks shy of her 90th birthday.

From national capital to capital city. 1 of 9 siblings.
First in Canada.
32 years old.
My grandmother walked 10k and back to work every day
until money came in for a bus pass.
My destiny was to work for people; there is no shame in that.

Straight from the airport he arrived at the couch of
570 Jameson Avenue.
3rd floor. Two bedrooms. 5 people.
It was 1967 and my father was fifteen.
I slept on that couch till '71.

"Baby Girl, Gayle. 1982"
- for Marsha

I.

If science had advanced more quickly,
If a god had seen to keep that acorn heart beating,
Do you think we would have shared a room?

Two twins in place of the double four-posted canopy under
which I slept until I left home.
Our names embossed on the wooden signs hanging
above our heads.

Would yours be among the list of names our
elders call out until they get the right one:
"Mel-Kar-Tas-Cha-Car-Zo-So-Marsha!"

There's a photo of our mom very pregnant in plaid. Her hair is
cropped very short, shorter than the curtain of curls in the
picture of her breastfeeding me.

She glides down the stairs. Hand on railing,
eyes cast forward,
over, and beyond the photographer's gaze.
Orange, green, red, yellow squares filling out the slope of her.

That's you in there.

Only 2 years apart.

I wish you could have been born with
a beating heart.
So accustomed to the long absences left
by death

I thirst for sister stories.
A couple years here.
A few there.

Tangible recollections of road trips,
birthday parties, inside jokes, and
pointless fights.

I'm missing the raw material
required to build nostalgic daydreams
Instead substituting ethereal fantasies of
what could
have been.

II.

Dressed in all black
sweating in summer heat
for someone else's burial I
begin to look for you.

Flagged by friends with deep-
set hearts we scour the
grounds for a sign a signal to
your resting place.

Heads down, cinched brows we
crunch over August grass
passing over others' lost little ones
a garden of the smallest souls.

Cherubs and rocking horses rendered
in granite
stand guard over their sleeping charges, serve as my guides
through the rows of crackling shrubbery.

All I have is a number.

When I finally find where you should be
flat turf greets me instead
I've checked and rechecked and know
this is the spot.

I begin to dig.

Tears slide into my downturned mouth
as my pocketknife strains to loosen the sod.
I wince as cold soil lodges under my fingernails,
a small mound gathering beside me.

The coverage cleared; I hold the buried brick heavy, cold, wet.
Thumbs caress grainy soil,
greet my nose with cut grass and dew drenched sidewalk.

I think of your breathless body and channel
what warmth I have into that stone
redirecting the swelter of my body heat
hovering over your submerged sarcophagus

Embossed with a number – the only proof that you're here,
I lay it atop the now upturned grass.
Feather your grave with whatever beauty I can find.

Portrait

I have spent so long shuttered behind homemade
curtains and fire doors.
The extrovert previously known buckled from the force
of this illness;
the introvert stretched their wings briefly
then wrapped them tight around their chest.

The portrait embedded into my skin had been mine alone
until now.
Mine to examine in the mirror and hold closely
Tracing the charcoal lines of her illustrated visage.

But here, under the hot Jamaican sun, my arms bare themselves
to the elements.
This new sunshine rolls over the bright ink and sharp lines,
the marigolds and memories of my mother's face.

In this estranged homeland, bodies are close, eyes scan and
settle on the features of my foreignness.
Tongues flap and unfurl in enquiry, out of wonder and
Christian incredulity.
Is that you? Who is it? Who is it.

I find myself overwhelmed with the repetitive answers of
"my mom" "died" dead" "alive? no" "when I was a kid".
The words become scuffed and leaden, as purposeless
as a cracked key.

The proclamation of my half-orphaning to strangers with whom it
will hold no prolonged weight claws small and jagged tears in the
quilted reminiscence swathing my body in memories.

For the first time, a flash of regret in the choice to inscribe myself
with mourning for all the world to see.
The gutting exhumation of her loss, the stinging, the burn
of each needle puncture
are mine to hold and weep over, and not for others to pry
into and touch.

Salty fingers tease my raw flesh.

Lottery Numbers

Dad's silence on her birthday told me
we don't talk about Mom here.
I stifled my questions and pretended
to forget the date while quietly
humming "Happy Birthday" under my
breath.

Late toddler to late twenties
secure believing he had cleared
his emotional archive and moved on.

I asked him about the lottery.

Something about the idea of
chance mixed with detailed strategy
has a decades-long hold on most of
my family.

My father plays the lottery every Friday.
One day I ask him how he's picked
out which numbers he would play.

he said: I've been playing
the same numbers since
1988.
1988 is the year my mother died.
when I ask what they were he
wrote and said:

3-8-15-51-18-25
3 for 3:00 a.m. when your mom died
8 Month of Aug.
15th floor of Women's College Hospital
51 room #

18-18th of Aug. the day of
25-25th of Aug. Funeral

Every Friday for 24 years.
A man forces himself to remember.
Every Friday a near-retired engineer
returns to an unthinkable equation with
no solution.

Mad Black

Residential Galapagos.
Paradise advertised on a daylight-dimmed neon sign on Dufferin.
Somewhere between nine and ten and I am finally sitting up in
bed which brings me that much closer to getting up, I think.

I don't know all of the stigma about being a Mad Black Woman
I know it is the kind of woman I must never let myself become.
And yet.
There are rumours.
Stories that my mother changed each full moon.
I never witnessed it and she, long dead, isn't here to ask.
I wonder constantly, was she ever Mad Black, like me?
Did she too stay in the dark, her could-fill-a-room face emptied
yet twinkling with salt crystals left from her tears?
I would ask but who would tell me the truth?

It has taken my lifetime to collect any overturned fossils
of fact about her.
Would anyone divulge a missive that wasn't perfect?
Maybe she didn't identify with the diagnoses, but living through
that measure of suffering carries a cost.
Now, I hold her traumas in my body, her losses, Her loss.
If only I could talk to her and ask her how she survived.

Finally losing it.
Seems a cliché that after all this time of trying to enclose this
catalogue of survivorship within myself my arms got too tired.
My muscles trembled into jelly before snapping,
hurling my now empty arms to my sides.
All of the me I'd been squeezing to my chest trying
not to drop fell to the floor.
Some pieces broke, sand and silica tumbleweeds
dashing across tiles.
Some rolled away, skating into endless shadows and obscurity.
Some burst – and dried into stains on the carpet.

I keep being advised, kindly, to go to the doctor to have this
situation taken care of.
But I know that this doctor has been looking at me with
feebly disguised skepticism
since my body started breaking down and I visited more and more.
He thought me crazy for insisting on tests that he never gave.
He said, "I wouldn't anticipate a cure" and went back to his notes.
I hope that this time I am strong enough to say no when he says
"I know best, not you",
and instead increases my dose.

I wore 3 bandages for 2 days to cover 19 cut-scars I made
in half as many minutes.

These days it is my boyfriend's razor broken out from
its three-blade case.
The best times were when so many tools were around.
A geometric compass for etching.
Lady Bics for speed,
my stepmother's manicure kit was an assassin's bounty.

When I was a kid, first starting this habit, my wrist was the
place to go.
The skin is so thin. The cuts so easy.
The thrill of catching a vein to make a real mess.
These days kids are smarter and more discreet: stomachs,
thighs, ankles.
Call me old fashioned.
Like running into someone you thought moved away,
whose return startles and soothes you.
I'm nostalgic for the feel and drag of cool steel
across decades-old scars
waiting for the pleasure of pressure release.
Call me Mad.
Call me Black.
I do.

Roaches in Daylight

it's only a couple
they're only in the kitchen
they're only in the kitchen
and the bathroom
they're only out at night
and during the day
it's not that bad.

we shower together
darting eyes and antennae twitch to the
movements of my nude and lathered body.

we cook together
I chop slowly, one eye on the board
the other scanning around in search of you.

I toss ingredients in the pot
and you dash across the counter
trying to make it to the drain before I

c r u s h.

I savour the crunch of your exoskeleton.

pausing before I lift my now landfilled spatula to expose
the smear of your remains leaking through the takeout napkin
now your shroud.

Scouring Craigslist ads for
decent
accessible
above-ground apartments
that I can afford.

Thought I found one.
But it's the unit across the
hall.
Conclusion - they don't exist.
Except for the roach riddled one I currently live in.

miscellaneous gadgetry

"I said to you honey just open your heart
when I have trouble even opening a honey jar"
– Joanna Newsome

Joanna Newsom writes the lines to supply the breaking open I
need to get to, to cry. these tunes are the muse at the core of the
ruse I play to pretend my wild emotions are subdued. when you
forget to eat until 4pm when your vision starts to blur. minute
movements thud brutishly, hammer lead into my limbs.

the only routine
I can manage is to trudge to my classes in an institution that
doesn't recognize the beauty of a broken body.

solitude is an echo chamber
a cycling self-injurious slide show
narrated by my night terrors
hypnotizing me into dissociation.

Hives

Sandpaper scales spread over
My already lamenting complexion
And I
Find myself wishing once more for the luxury
of white scars.

Instead, shadows multiply in pace with
Skin-weeping sores
litter me, lichen barnacles.

Pulling at collars.
Each pass by the mirror
Another mock against perfection.

Grin at me from beneath my skin.

Little Imps.

Bloodflame

I want to set my uterus on fire
is a thought I used to have
as razors ripped apart my organs and
split the middle hemisphere of my brain

imagining a lit cauldron
of flesh and fire
a balm for my
untenable anguish

I want to set my uterus on fire
is a thought I harbour now when
I open my closet
and see it floating in its
formaldehyde urn

I needed to see it
to hold it to say
goodbye
apparently

I thought I would keep it out on a shelf
where it would serve as a reminder of
what, exactly

I didn't want the MIC[1]
to have any more of me
than it had already taken

I want to burn it now
phantom cramps and spasms
remind me
I haven't dealt with my losses

How to grieve all that left my life that year?
Uterine ashes into art

---

1   medical industrial complex

IV

SCAB. PICK. SCAB.

gather seeds of promise
chew one for each broken vow
water to germinate

I Fell Asleep in My Party Dress

Kept it on for my morning phone calls, teeth brushing, emptying litter, applying for jobs.

It makes me feel fancy.

"There's something about Saturday nights that make me feel like kissing"

said to Brescia in front of Unit 2, Sat. Aug 10, 2013.

Sad Clown Saxophone

New Year's morning
makeup and hair still done.
Instead of hot queer I read
saxophone*
I woke up in all of my clothes under my sheets the lights on.

I'm tucked in and there's no one to have it done it but me.
Still drunk only slept for five hours but the morning is beast time
dog out
dog in
water
tea
tylenol
pats
cats
back to bed.

New Year's night
showered
sweats
more tea
toast
back to bed
all clean except for the saxophone remnants on my pillow

*composed using Dragon Dictate which interpreted "sad clown" as
saxophone.

cheshire cat moon

cheshire cat moon rests her dents on the lens of
my specs a tiny glimmer, a hint above my rims eyes
instead focussed on the road just ahead of my
handlebars

How to Fold a Fitted Sheet and Other Things I Never Learned From My Mother

In a recent trip to the Laundromat
       Crammed into scrunched gathers
              I found myself.

Down The House

is the green tiles in my grandma's bathroom.
walls, floor, tub and toilet all a matching shade of what must have
been sold as "avocado"

is the smell of cinnamon flavoured toothpaste blended with bars
of Irish Spring, bought in bulk a decade ago.
I checked and the toothpaste expired in 2006.

the taste of varnished wood crushed into the spaces between my
teeth as I chewed her cherry bed frame.
gnaw-marks and faded initials etch scars across the foot board
where I rested my chin to watch the Price is Right and YnR.

night jasmine swirling through the window screen

familiar pilling of overused comforters, textile goose bumps brush
themselves across my calves.

growing older and realizing that house will soon disappear from
our family map.

never having an electric drier, home is the coarse and crispy
comfort of her line-dried towels. scented faintly of vinegar – to
keep them soft.

snapshots of my growing body as I stood before the full-length
mirror in the hall over the years. revelling in only child amusement
I would suck in my belly or puff out my cheeks, trying on different
selves that no one else could see.

My Grandmother Keeps Losing Her Teeth

Not the ones she was born with, those were replaced long ago.
According to her, the teeth God gave her leapt out her head
the moment she moved to this country.
Happened to her brother too.

She has two teeth missing in the front.
One on top and one on the bottom.

First one she lost eating pork chops –
she swears she wasn't gnawing on the bone
like she usually does but I am not so sure.

The next one fell right out of her mouth when she was brushing
her teeth.

She won't go to church until they're fixed because she claims
it's just too unsightly to open her mouth looking like that in the
House of God.

She tried to cuss out the phone company but couldn't say
Stupidity because of the holes and that just made her angrier.

She says once they go back in she'll be more careful and maybe
won't grind her bones into pulp like she always does.

I don't believe her
I don't care
I don't know another way to eat them

mango threads in my teeth

draping my upper body over the arm of the chair to avoid dripping
nectar down the front of myself. leaning forward, I stretch my
neck and tilt my head down as to prevent the honeyed juice
from careening down my chin and onto my clothes. manners
grown in a Black house in a white town where assimilation was
more important than preservation and Keeping Up Appearances
was a rule as well as a PBS rewatch, I am uncomfortable eating
with emotional abandon. burying my face into the tart, stringy
pulp. gnashing front teeth into bitter, waxen skin. tearing the
membrane from the now revealed flesh and giving in to the sweet
and sour halo forming around my lips the closer I get to the pit,
seems salaciously divine.
still, I proceed with caution.

I Would Come Out Tonight...

lost in my closet
knee deep
in the seasonal detritus
of dyke march costumery

try not to tear as I
tear off the
short shorts
low cut
high tops

try not to trip as I
rip off the
button up
skinny jeans
ironic suspenders

try to outlast as I
pass on the
comfy jeans
plain tee
blundstones

which me do I resemble when
I assemble
this
apparently celebratory
ensemble?

already a nail-biter on a good
day
this annual
identity dialogue with
my full-length panic

wears my soles paper
thin before hitting
asphalt in dissolve

swift decision making
show off my sexy self or
blow off
oh-so familiar irritants of
a big ol' gay party

over-entitled sweaty white butches who
sloshing tent beer on my kicks
special for the occasion
admire my

exotic-erotic
unplanned-tan
and alluringly
unconventional outer shell

who
sidle up beside
instantly decide
my self, sexy
is theirs to clutch, grasp, kiss
and touch without a whisper of
yes

staring at the me-sized glass echo
I banish the impulse to
paper-bag-princess the whole thing
and smile at how this
Pride
in the end just makes me want
to hide.

V

SCAR. HEAL. GROW.

untether soul strings
stretch fingers, toes, mouth, eyes
scream and breathe, repeat.

Qrip Love

heard about it whispered across Wi-Fi walls
that ethereal spark that comes from
the secret satisfaction of qrip[2] love

---

2   queer + crip (sick, disabled, mad identified)

nice to meet you

nice to meet you.
how many languages do I speak these
words?
N T M Y
flat hands together
#1 handshape together
point
inhale
sip
smudge
exhale

purple roots, soft leaves
cut above ground
lay in boiled water
not boiling
be gentle with the fronds
this leaf grows this way here but not
there
what does this medicine look like
where your roots grow?

washed lightly in soft smoke healing
my meditation glitches to the photo of a
brightly lit white, blonde, and blue woman
smile stretched across her colonizing face

her caption shouts the anticipation for her new
book about 'herbal healing wands'
'smudging rituals' it's called
white people are so skilled at ruin.

at home, I open my door to the hazy
sweetness of sandalwood
my dead mom's favourite,
so says her last living bestie.

in the after swallow of this tea
sage and sweetgrass
an earthy tang recalls cerasee and senna
to my tongue a nervine bitterness
dark jewel-toned elixir, more malachite than
emerald
a darkness rich in tonic and temporality
so many stories to undo.

Vinyl Spine

Once
down on a time
when young bodies
pressed into each other
more or less with each
change of the beat

To and fro
But always close

Smile and writhe under dimmed lighting
Fingers pushing upwards and clapping along

Dance

Not to music anymore because the chatter sound
scuffle sound of
hundreds of small talk meet-cutes and
hundreds of well-worn sneakers rise above the hi-fi

To and fro
But always close
Heels crushing toes and knees grazing thighs
our bodies meld into each other, sugar crystals into syrup

We spread ourselves all over one another

We come from work, school, home if we have one
Some plucked right from fucking in each other's beds
The damp, sharp, reek of sex breathes itself out of our fingers
mouths to dance too,
with the thick and salty-sweet air hung low above our heads

To and fro
But always close

Once down on a
time
Swaying, shaking
Grinding, never-minding
with my eyes closed
this
is
my
jam!

Involuntary shoulder rolling, two-stepping
chest booming airwaves
hoist me out of my seat, into the throng
a long time
ago

Now.
Balance-shaky back-achy, rising with effort for one
song.
Take a break and snake my way onto the floor for
more of the movement my muscles remember
but can seldom recreate.

To and fro
But always

Along with coal blackened eyes and plum purple lips
I practice my finest nonchalance
announcing that I
don't mind at all leaning
against this wall.

This shame-able-bodied daydream
pushes my two feet forward and leaves
my third at home.
It packs me full of percs and vodka and
swirls

of smoke, to stifle
the life from the
bent, barbed nails pierced
into my fierce and fighting body
pulsing to the rhythm but
too sore to stand.

My back against cool concrete,
I face the crowd – one heaving breathing organism.
One hand on my cane the other drags a ripped and
wobbling chair, vintage vinyl holds up my spine all
cinched and creaking.

Cane between my knees the
rings on my fingers bounce
lights around and through faces
two feet higher than my own.

Now these multitude of grounding pillars
send pulses of drums into my knees
along my thighs and this dance just grew
more invigorating.

To and fro
But always close to the floor
and stretching the wretched up
and out of
my hips, round my shoulders
explode out of my fists 'cross
my tits pounding this beat
down from the air back into my
feet.

Rise

If only in the morning silences, you are breath steadily falling
between my uneven exhales.
Muted dreaming.
Sunrise whispers broken by sprinkles of sparrow-song.
Here, no dawn sun bleeds into the river you etch into my skin
your workworn fingertips
Mapping canyons and vales into my landscape.
Eyelids tight
Taste buds tickle eyelashes and shiver giddily you return the favour
Each turn, sway, rock your limbs provoke releases new shadows
that
battletango as light carves small splashes along deep corridors.

Deli Counter

Stunned, chest rhythm rising as
Your dimples emerged, winking and elastic as you greeted the
attendant.

"Two hundred grams of artichokes."

I liked your taste for brined hearts
Pictured you leaning over a steaming pot peeling
Away coarse
Petal by Petal
Until you reached the soft core.

I smiled.

You shot one back, teeth gleaming
and my breath caught
In my throat.
When I asked what else you were getting you stepped closer.
Pupil to pupil, golden green met midnight brown
And I imagined us feeding each other morsels of the prosciutto
now warming in my hand.

Bid farewell, said happy eating
And as you wandered tapping melons and squeezing
pears I pondered over our chance encounter.

Eyes closed,
Leaning my blushing cheek against the freezer door
I ran my tongue over my teeth and tasted the last
Bite
Of cured meat from your fingertips.

Sing Song

the first time i remember hearing your voice
i was lying on the ultramarine blue carpet of
my grandmother's living room.

the second time i remember hearing your voice
i was lying in the bed of one of your sisters
talking, laughing, storytelling literal lifetimes of new-to-each-
other knowledge

she said my name and i heard you

the third time i remember hearing your voice
i was lying in my bed with my cats i called
them to me, come 'ere, you said.

with <3

Thinking of and thanking you
for allowing me to be with you and your body.

The kind of inside that is beyond
wet, warm, flesh where I can trace the ridges
and walls of your rippling pathway with my fingertips

Softly outline the firm, pulsating ring - a gateway.

Your body upon entering
guides me through mazes of sinew and hot blood vessels,
thrashing against the membrane
that separates them from my wandering fingers.

A vast and intricate system of passageways,
each turn I take ripples through your body.

Pressure rising, the kinetic zap exhales
with your breath in halted gasps
and growling moans.

I melt for the expression
on your face as you dip into my depths, into the
pools of anticipation waiting for your touch.

I pour my joy down your fingers, into your palm,
and marvel at how smoothly our bodies combine into each other.

I imagine a morning in the future
when our lives and homes
make room for us
to wake up unrobed and enraptured
next to one another.

Our few feverish nights
like lightening

illuminate each element of life
around me

Gray days brighten slightly
when I spot the rays of our
lovesun
peeking through the clouds.

Saccharine snapshots keep me affection receptive
replenish my stockpile of reasons
to stick around when every other cerebral suggestion
instructs otherwise.

Squeals of rampant glee
mix with my perma-panic upon realizing that –

Shit,

I really care for this person.

Enter an even more erratic panic at the thought that

Shit,

She really likes me too!

Well over a year since singledom.
since shedding a 6-year snakeskin.

The prospect of a long-term liaison
dances around and in front of us,
waiting for
the right moment to settle deeply between
our pressing palms.

Illness begets patience and I am in no rush.

I relish when our pain-drained bodies find their way together
each motion, made with intention
and for the first time
I find myself lying next to a body
who mirrors my own in its
complications.

With each date we discover paths
to our own access intimacy.

I look forward to learning everything that causes you pain,
as much as pleasure and
sharing the same secrets
with you.

Mapping a private cartography to each other's

tender points
            trigger points
                        hot spots
and no-zones.

Trading fibro files over
tea coffee Greek fries
nursing babies willful
toddlers.

The magnificent mess of our lives.

I'd say I can't wait but
I can.

Because the excitement of you
is almost as glorious as the reward
of your warmth
next to mine.

2050

No basements.
No attics.
No stairs of any kind.
A room for sleep.
A room for work.
A room to gather.
A room for visitors.
A room for sun.
A garden.
A tree or more.
In rhythm to season.
No highways.
No condos.
No neighbours too near.
Places for feast and for fire.
Spaces for board games and game plans
for justice.
Beast and bird aplenty.
Kin-made adornments through every doorway.
A me-made creation facing each direction.
So be it. See to it.[3]

---

3   quote by Octavia E. Butler

...at rest...
–for granny

they lay still, quiet
remembering each life they had lived
had warmed with honey throughout
their earth lifetime.

the crystalline obsidian sand shifted gently underneath
their body
warm licks of salt water flicked their ankles.

just beyond the opening of the hollow
where they awaited their transition a
leaping ring of fire kept company with
their long legacy of kin
come to make
offerings for their journey.

skin thin, soft and cascading upon itself
from age and ascendance.
all around
their body
beasts and creatures of all
sorts cushioned the aged frame in
gratitude for the care received
and in
support of their coming path.

a pack of spirits and guides
connected with them since before
their earth birth and who will remain
after their ancestor ascendance.

at their most boundless
most deliberate
most intentional
most cared for
and most whole self,
transformed into stardust
particles dispersed on
a slumbering sigh
whispers soaring away
on the wind atoms
rising into ancestor.

To: mel
Fr: your indestructible self

you have been a witch all along.

indifferent to the hushed cascade within an hourglass
unbothered by most, enlivened by masses
gathered together with kin, safely disguised from outer
observation
solid and heavy like your rock collection
that evolved into a crystal collection
a gem affinity

remember the gold
and the butterfly goo

forget voices claiming binaries as the only available option
forget voices insisting your creative curiosity was a pastime,
not a calling.
release the repeated rhetoric declaring you not smart
enough to understand
anything technological.
you are technology.

remember, i can feel you remembering
the dandelions, thistles, clovers, whistle grass, nettles, pinecones,
sap, ants, worms
the alchemy of sun through glass
the formula for melting chocolate with an easy-bake oven
the first time you knew ghosts were real, and with you

remember the wounds you opened so that you could learn,
so that you could teach yourself
how to heal them

remember bookcases crowned with dried bouquets
desiccated proof that someone at some time was proud of you
go back and look on the bookshelf
unicorns, sign language, criminal justice, vampires and other
melancholic macabre
all before you left at seventeen

remember the times when rules about your aesthetic, affection,
and after-school hours dared to dull your luminescence
remember, with life-learned knowledge
you would still find your way through
the cracks of those boxes

you have been a witch all along.

To my complex-bodied, jumble-minded,
neuro-divine beloveds...
To my niblings by blood and other bonds.
And to my younger self, thank you for
persisting me into existence.

fin.

Acknowledgements

To my mother, whose life and leaving became my call to poetic service.
To my grandmother who believed in my dream of having a book to hold in our hands one day.
To my dad for finally coming around to my weird, mostly.
To my friends and families who have encouraged me to keep going because they want to read what I've been scribbling in notebooks all this time.

To the original keepers of the lands I wrote and lived these poems on – the Huron-Wendat, Anishinaabe, Petun, Mississaugas of New Credit, Ohlone, Métis, Dakota, Cree and Oji-Cree, Dene as well as my Taino and Arawak ancestors. And to the Tr'ondek Hwech'in first nation on whose land these poems found their way together and back to me.

Thank you to Debra and everyone at Radiant Press; and to my lovingly brilliant editor Suzette Mayr. Thank you for welcoming me and for giving these pages a home.

To my teachers, possibility models, heartminders and other supporters on this journey, including but not limited to my beasts living and left, Anu Radha Verma, Sarah Pinder, Simone Schmidt, Kate Atkinson, The Lady Ms. Vagina Jenkins, DS; Siblings living and left; Austin Epema, Chris Abani, Sharanpal Ruprai, Margaret Christakos, Lillian Allen, Dionne Brand, Audre Lorde, Octavia E. Butler, nayirrah waheed, Yrsa Daley Ward, Alexis Pauline Gumbs, Almah LaVon and Dark Sciences fam, Not Lost Workshop groups, Charm Torres, Free Woman, Naimonou James, Bani Amor, Alexis 'One Ancient Soul' Jones, Jade T. Perry, Slow Waves kin, medicinal plants, black tea, treats, same foods, dreams and intuition.

m. patchwork monoceros is a poet and interdisciplinary artist exploring polysensory production and somatic grief through text/ile and film. Their work considers a collective qrip (queer+crip) consciousness by connecting to marvelous bodies living with complexity as sick or disabled. A Black creator of Jamaican Taino/Arawak ancestry, monoceros lives with their four-legged menagerie: Onion, Dax, Hoa and Essun in Treaty 1 also known as Winnipeg, MB, traditional territory of the Anishinaabe, Dene, Cree, Dakota and Oji-Cree Nations and home of the Métis First Nation.